For all my loved ones, especially mum, my biggest and brightest cheerleader.

I may have yet failed to capture you in a poetic work of art, but know you will be forever captured in my heart.

Ordinary, Precious and Wild

Amy Samouelle

BookLeaf
Publishing

Ordinary, Precious and Wild © 2023 Amy Samouelle

All rights reserved.

Amy Samouelle asserts the moral right to be identified as author of this work.

Presentation by *BookLeaf Publishing*

Web: www.bookleafpub.com

E-mail: info@bookleafpub.com

ISBN: 9789357442800

First edition 2023

ACKNOWLEDGEMENT

Inspiration comes from many places, but most of my poetry is about people and relationships and just the act of being human and alive. I am grateful for all the experiences I have had that have led me to where I am now.

I must credit poets Mary Oliver and Robert Frost for inspiring a couple of my lines and the various friends and family who are included in this collection.

PREFACE

I was tired of hearing myself say how much I wanted to "write more poetry" and this challnege forced my hand. If you feel the same about any aspect of your life, I'd say just go for it! Put yourself and your work out there. My style is uncomplicated and not overly poetic, much like me and my life and it was important to me to remain authentic and real. I hope others will relate to the themes and enjoy reading these poems as much as I enjoyed the creative process of writing them.

Solitude

Swan

Off-grid for a while

Lean

Into

This

Uncomplicated existence

Daydream

Emerge transformed

Knowing

She knows she knows

she has a talent for rollerblading.

A preference for marmalade

over jam.

She knows how to whistle through her fingers

and make love to a man.

She knows she doesn't know

how to knit, or bake, or sew.

Or crisp up roasties

quite like her nan's.

She knows she's useless with chopsticks

and can't be relied on to make plans.

What she doesn't know

and others can see clearly

is that she makes people feel at ease

and she's loved and appreciated dearly.

She's also unaware

that she talks over people when excited.

Crinkles her nose when uncertain

and can offer advice uninvited.

No one yet knows what her future will hold.

That tomorrow, she'll conceive her first child.

Her life will be far from perfect

but it will be real, and precious, and wild.

Becoming

Out of the shadows

and into the light

You came to the fore

without a fight

in the end.

From unknown, to unseen

to seen, to known

You made yourself at home in my bones

and I dared let you!

And that made all the difference.

Scribbles

I long to scribble like a child.

A crayon, gripped in my pudgy fist.

No rules.

Just random chaos on the page.

Growth

The gap between stimulus and response is
growing.

Today I chose silence over snark.

And with it came an inner knowing

that light is emerging where there used to be
dark.

Yoga

She savours the stretch

Spine arched like a cat.

Then she rounds, and grounds

and greets the mat.

Inhaling slowly.

Letting go.

Releasing resistance.

Finding flow.

Creating more space in her inner world

she can take up more space in the outer world.

She moves how she means

and means how she moves.

Getting out of those familiar grooves

and into her own lane.

Advice

Everyone wants to fix the problem

Make it better

Patch it up

Tell you what the answer is

But wait a second…

What's the question?

Surely that's a better place to start.

Make it go away

Plaster on a smile

you'll be okay

"yes, yes, you'll be fine"

"My advice is X, Y Z(ee)"

"You should… blah..blah… 1,2,3"

"Have you tried this?"

"Why not try that?

"If I were you, I'd get a cat!"

I know you mean well

but you're not me

and I never asked for your advice.

I've just opened up about feeling lonely

Isn't it clear, I'm looking for connection?

Some conversational ease

A meaningful conversation- please!

And just so you know

Cats make me sneeze.

Loneliness

Esther sank

feeling forlorn.

Her chair sagging comfortably

around her deflated form.

It carried her weight

knew her fears

All her regrets

and half-baked ideas.

A sigh escaped as she settled in for the night

Resigned as the day is to fade with the light.

And again tomorrow

A new sorrow.

Late Pandemic Summer

It was a warm summers day

Mum got stung by a bee.

We'd cycled to see you

Sat in your garden

with cups of tea.

I don't remember what was said

except that there was laughter.

That was the last time I saw you.

Though I wouldn't know that

until after...

No one could guess what the future would bring

that sunny mid-summers day

I wish that I could have hugged you

as we rode our merry way.

(Remembering Barry Cater)

A special bond

"The more people I meet,

the more I love my dog"

is a phrase well-worn

but earnestly meant.

I had that quote framed for him

one Christmas.

He's retired now.

Doesn't know many people.

A few acquaintances maybe

But he'll take them or leave them.

When I was 9,

and he was drunk

and we were camping

he told me he loved his dog more than he'd ever
loved another human.

"including me" I remember thinking.

I watch him sometimes

Struggle to connect to me- his daughter

Yet he shares a secret love language with his
dogs.

A bond

That will never be broken.

For my friends who are struggling right now

I don't know what to say.

And then I remind myself

that I don't have to know

or say

anything.

I just want you to know

that I'm here.

A listening ear.

And…

Nothing else much

Other than I hope things get easier in time

and you rediscover your shine.

On Leadership

You lit up the way

like you lit up the room

So that we could see the path.

I chose to start going

and follow my knowing

and I've never once looked back.

Rising above

I don my metaphorical armour

and step into the fray

I refuse to be dragged into drama

No thank you

Not today.

Housemates

I was happily hoovering the house

just hours after you'd gone.

Sucking away the last trail of crumbs and debris.

Teasing long clumps of your hair out of the
hoover head

and plug holes

Relishing the fact that it would be the last time
I'd have to do

this horrible job!

The echo of your last guitar solo still hung in the
air

I found myself humming along

"You'll be my Pixie Queen…"

I remember you filming yourself, strumming
away in our tiny kitchen

whilst I tried to cobble together lunch.

You were always in the way.

Increasingly frustrated

I clattered headfirst into an open cupboard.

Then proceeded to casually boil my egg

like nothing had happened.

Now, in the hallway,

I turn off the hoover

sit on the floor

and laugh out loud at the recording

that captured that moment

You, oblivious- until you watched it back.

Oh, how we howled!

Later, hoovering under your bed, I find that grubby cap of yours.

Dusting it off, I read:

"suicidal tendencies"

The band.

But it gets me thinking

of the night we started out playing an innocuous game of Scrabble

which somehow evolved into something deeper.

And how you never really know what demons

other people are facing.

As much as the past 7 months had been challenging for me

adjusting to your chaotic ways

and larger than life personality

It was made known that I was appreciated

at a time when you were struggling

more than I perhaps knew.

I was your friend

And though I doubt I'll be your friend forever

At this moment

In our history

It was enough.

(For Ben)

Morning Ritual

6am and it's cold and black

All is quiet on our cul-de-sac.

Until a pipe slowly gurgles

the heating kicks in

I peel back the duvet

Let the day begin.

Padding to the bathroom

barely awake

I'm tailed by my shadow

who likes to partake

In our morning ritual

My first wee of the day

A little game we've come to play.

One circuit through, and around each leg.

Then flop down to her back and beg.

I fuss her until my pee runs dry

then she's had enough

and says her goodbye.

Every morning

the same retreat

Wipe

Flush

Tomorrow, repeat.

Partnership

Ground is fertile

Roots are strong

Each day

Growing together

(For Greg)

Avoidance

I hear you running

your pounding feet

your steadfast adherence

Thrum thrum

to the beat

I watch you running

running away

running away from the ghosts of the day

You run from the truth

and you run from the pain

far, far away from your demons and your shame

There's always someone else to blame

So you run and run

'til everything's numb

Diligently dodging discomfort

But I still see you.

Dear reader

I hope you don't mind

if I share this poem with you.

It's just a few words I hashed together.

Nothing special.

Probably a load of guff.

Don't worry if you don't get the chance to read
it.

It isn't really "poemy" enough.

Self image

I skittered across the frosty decking

feeling a first-class fool

in my pink woolly hat

and polka dot bikini

All goose pimpled limbs

pale against the starlight.

Sinking into the heat of the water

I parted ways with my body

A shedding of a skin that had never fitted

Never fitted in...

All I could do is watch in wonder

as I floated up, up and away

to disappear with the steam

Tendrils that coiled out of sight into the night.

A glassy lake, gargantuan and regal

was flanked by rows of snow-capped firs

and reflected the light of a billion twinkling
stars.

Stillness

and

Peace

My perpetually racing mind ceased.

Reels of images of my self, my body, my image, my worth, my beauty

paled in comparison to the raw, unfiltered beauty

that surrounded me that night

and I realised deep in my marrow

that it's all just an illusion.

I made a choice then to free myself from the collusion

and just be me

Just BE

It was profound

I was lost in the moment

But I knew too, I was found.

Weather watcher

Today she feels agile

raring to go.

But last Tuesday she was fragile

stuck on go slow.

Her emotions are the weather

clouds passing by.

She's started to watch them

float over her sky.

She's practicing non-judgement

and getting curious too.

Chronic illness is wearing

she needs something to do.

A new perspective

so a weather watcher she's become.

Trying to detect when she starts to feel glum.

Realising when she resists

and wills herself schtum

that those thoughts just persist

banging their drum.

When she looks up at grey skies

and decides to complain

she finds herself stuck under pouring rain.

and hyper focused on all her pain...

So instead she'll look up at her sky

stop interfering and asking "why?"

Stop prodding the clouds

until they darken and multiply

and swallow every inch of her clear blue sky.

Because that's when the present moment is lost
in commotion

She's allowed herself to be hijacked by old
thoughts and emotion.

It's harder for her then to see a way ahead
clearly

And pave her path towards what matters really.

I'm proud of her for doing this work

A responsibility that many shirk.

She's getting wiser every day

And the weather?

All is calm

At least for today.

Seedling

Curiosity tugs

Hesitant, I sniff the air

An opportunity is out there

No longer time to play safe

Growing pains have become too hard to ignore

Everything, is in store.

Milton Keynes UK
Ingram Content Group UK Ltd.
UKHW010759110923
428455UK00015B/849